TELLING

MOMENTS

15 GAY MONOLOGUES

Applause Acting Series

TELLING MOMENTS

15 GAY MONOLOGUES

By Robert C. Reinhart

APPLAUSE
NEW YORK • LONDON

AN APPLAUSE ORIGINAL

TELLING MOMENTS
15 GAY MONOLOGUES
By Robert C. Reinhart

© COPYRIGHT 1994 Applause Theatre Books

Inquiries regarding performance rights should be addressed to the author, care of the Doyle Agency, 865 First Avenue, New York, N.Y. 10017

Library of Congress Catalog-in-Publication Data

Reinhart, Robert C.
    Telling moments : 16 gay monologues / by Robert C. Reinhart.
        p.   cm. — (Applause acting series)
      1. Gay men — Drama. 2. Monologues. I. Title. II. Series.
    PS3568.E4924T45   1994
    812' .54--dc20   93-45366
                                               CIP

British Library Catalog-in-Publication Data
A catalogue record for this book is available from the British Library

APPLAUSE BOOKS
211 W. 71ST STREET
NEW YORK, NY 10023
PHONE: 212-595-4735
FAX: 212-721-2856

406 Vale Road
Tonbridge KENT TN9 1XR
PHONE: 0732 357755
FAX: 0732 770219

First Applause Printing: 1994

DEDICATION

Too many voices in my life have been stilled by AIDS. So many gaping silences where there should be familiar greetings, some good gossip, trivia, and a few much needed laughs. This book of "voices" is in memory of theirs.

It is also for my nephew Gary and for Chris, both of whom I love, value and admire.

My thanks to these very talented people who so generously helped in the evolution of these monologues in performances at New York's The Kitchen and Kaufman Theatre: Peter Bartlett, Tracy Davis, Michael Delaney, Timothy Kivel, Jim Peacock, Peter Sentkowski, Eric Tull, and Richard Woods.

CONTENTS

INTRODUCTION

In the mid-fifties a friend played Ruth Draper's *The Italian Lesson* for me and marked my imagination forever. Draper's voice alone evoked the character's past, present and future and furnished my mind with a lavish set, wonderful costumes, perfect lighting, and about a dozen other characters I could have described in detail, even though none of them had a line. My sense of theatrical possibility grew vast.

Ever since that first hearing, Draper's work has served me as a "master class" in monologue writing and an ongoing lesson in humility.

But if Draper was the preeminent practitioner of the form in the fifties, she wasn't the only soloist: Cornelia Otis Skinner wrote and played in "Paris '90," Elsa Lanchester toured in her "Roundabout" show of songs and monologues, and the sweetly funny Joyce Grenfell came often to New York to enchant and beguile. Interestingly—and oddly—there were no men working with the form in that period.

Then, about two decades later, Hal Holbrook and James Whitmore brought us Mark Twain and Will Rogers, and the form was not only resuscitated but went on to even greater vitality and variety, and hasn't lost any steam since.

My fascination with monologues continues, probably because there are few things that are more fun to write or to see played well. The form also serves my preference for minimal scenery and props. It also satisfies my deep, affection for actors who often astound me with their evocative powers and who seem to enjoy a chance to venture solo onto the high wire.

This collection is labeled gay, because all the men are

attracted to other men. Other than noting that affectional distinction, all I can say is that I hope these pieces provide pleasure to readers, players and hearers.

Bob Reinhart
New York City

PRODUCTION NOTES

THE ACTORS: *Telling Moments* offers several options for actors; the monologues can be performed by three actors as a complete one-act entertainment or done singly for entertainment or auditions. When performed in its entirety, three actors are needed; one in his early or mid-twenties, one anywhere from his thirties to early forties, and one at any age beyond fifty.

THE PLAYING ENVIRONMENT: The playing area can be proscenium or in-the-round. A chair, stool or box is needed for sitting. Props should be dictated by absolute necessity. That is, props should only be used when it would be clumsy or too artful not to. Dark shirts and trousers are all the costume needed.

Only lighting defines playing areas and helps set the mood. For instance, the atmosphere of Stafford's beach house would be enhanced by the use of clear sunny lighting, the bar by the use of color, the talk-show interview by light shifts.

THE SEQUENCE: Although the pieces are presented in the order in which they were performed, they can be played in any sequence that best suits the needs of a production and cast.

ACTING NOTES

There are some possibilities and "actor's traps" in these monologues that are worth pointing out. In general, even when the character might seem to invite dislike or condescension, that is never the intention. Each is written in an effort at understanding the person, even when they don't seem to understand themselves. If the players learn to like and understand the characters, audiences can draw their own conclusions.

No character is written to evoke pity and to play to that invites disaffection, not a little boredom and, worst of all, is a sure way to kill a laugh.

The characters are driven by the great energizers of anger, avarice, need, fear and love—or, in some cases, what passes for them.

To quickly run down the men in *Telling Moments*:

STAFFORD: Most important, he is not epicene. He is successful and competent. He is trying to impress—and seduce—the young man in ways that usually work for him. The young man is simply "this week's model," the new bit of jewelry he wlll dangle for his friend's admiration.

ARNOLD: This is one pissed-off man. He's furious with his defecting lover and equally enraged at himself for being a damned fool, for tying up the loose ends of their life together while his former lover vacations with his replacement.

FRANCIS: This is a man "on the turn," just beyond being motivated by faith and becoming only a caretaker of ritual and property. He fears looking within, so aims his feelings at what he sees around him. His life is a perilous balancing act.

EDDIE: He's an inept Scheherazade. He's trying

desperately to be beguiling, so he can stay where it feels safe, warm and good. But he's failing and he senses it, which only makes him try harder as he plunges on with his stories.

PHIL: His letter is impelled by anger, not begging, and he hates feeling put in the position of explaining himself to someone who should not require he justify himself.

LUDLOW: The director is a distaught kindergarten teacher, but very serious about his art. Don't wink or jab the audience in the ribs. Let them find the gags.

TOBY, HANK AND LEONARD: This is essentially musical in its rhythm and rehearsal should reveal the tempo and pitch. The tone is cool, almost formal, told the way most men tell war stories.

CHRIS: He's making the very hard decision to pay to tell a truth in public he's sure will make him look foolish.

BRENDAN: Age doesn't dim passionately acquisitive natures. If you are a young player, don't use a wobbly voice to indicate age. Older men rarely develop fragilely unsure voices, any more than they wear baggy cardigans.

DANA: He lives by calculated charm. He has developed a bantering professional ease that has greased his way to the fringes of someone else's affluence. He no longer dares show resentment or disaffection. He was an actor; he still is. His last line ("What future?") can be played either of two ways; with the edged irony of lost expectations or with an offhand bantering tone that just misses insouciance.

RICHARD: The lover to whom he is talking is one more unruly piece of a "corporate" life that needs managing. He never does hit the right note of sincerity, it's more as if he's losing an account than a lover. He doesn't know that what works in business can be murderous in private life.

DES: This is a trick, and a tough one. He's the talk show

guest whose eyes—and brain—go wandering off from too many inane questions.

NICK, TREVOR AND CORY: Three living illustrations of "The Fine Art of Sinking Yourself" or "How to Sleep Solo."

TELLING MOMENTS

THE MONOLOGUES

TUNING UP
THE COMPANY

—My parents would sooner support me as an ax murderer than a ballet dancer.

—All night long he kept saying, "Ted, I love you." My name is Bill.

—I'm starting to read between the lines on birthday cards.

—This is probably the first time in history that impotence is a medical asset.

—Yes, but can he love a fireman?

—If I were interviewing me for life today, I wouldn't hire me.

—Hē *says* muscles bore him, but...

—I should have left him at the dog food counter where I met him.

—It was closing time, I was a little drunk, so I went right up to him and said, "Look, I'm sorry I called you ugly at midnight."

—He leaves me and I gain forty pounds and a Lhasa Apso.

—If *he* had a baby it would take an oral surgeon to deliver it.

(*As voices above progress, lights fade up on players. Lights are up full, as next lines are heard.*)

—Lou, I have a big favor to ask. Will you come over Saturday and help me pack his shit. I know I don't have to ask, but the more painfull I can make this for myself, the sooner I'll get around to hating the bastard.

—Well, he's French, Mrs. Samuels, so make something

with innards. The French always seem to like the unspeakable bits of cows.

—Hey, Stappy, get your dumb ass over here. Not him. He's the King of Crisco. Try the guy in the green shirt. He's OK Gets his pants off and passes out.

—Say ten "Our Fathers" and ten "Hail Marys" and make a firm commitment not to do it again. In nomine patris, et filii, et spiritus sanctus, amen. The confessions of ten-year-olds are very peculiar.

—I lost fifteen pounds on location. Nothing fits. I don't want you to fly your tailor out, I want to go home to Ben. I know the tour's in my contract, but... Have you seen the rough cut? It's cinema's answer to the tse-tse fly.

—The nurse says you're not dying, Donny. I know you're seventy-nine. No, I don't expect you to live forever. And you've already told me the medicine gives you erections. No, I don't want to see it.

—We'll be eighty-five for dinner, Geoffrey. Mr. Farringer will be fifty-three but, for God's sake, don't tell him I told you or he'll feel the fifteen thousand he spent on his lift is right down the drain.

—He's moving in.

—He's moving out.

—I wish he'd move.

THE TROUBLE WITH BEACHES
STAFFORD

Phew! Be a love and open the doors. It smells awful in here. I hope that doesn't mean that Mrs. Higgins hasn't been here. She's supposed to come Thursdays, but God knows when she really shows up or how long she stays. I would think that for sixty-five dollars a week she could spend some time here. There's little enough for her to do. I mean, how dirty can a beach house get?

Put your things in my room. 'Fraid you'll have to bunk in with me. Full house this weekend. Be a dear and take my bag, too.

No, my dear, that door, the master bedroom.

Hang your things with mine. And don't crush the clothes together; silk wrinkles so easily in this damp salt air. Then come help me move the plants. I want to put them so they're in the way, then I might remember to do something about them. I'm fond of plants, it's just finding the time to do something with the damned things.

Christ, there's the phone already. Be a love and when you're finished unpacking, would you mind putting the groceries away. (Hello. Be right with you.) No, forget everything else and make us a drink. Super-dry martini for me. Have what you want. There's tons of everything under there.

Hello. How did you know I was here? You lurking in your window again? I haven't had the time to sit down. Yes, isn't he? René. French. I met him at Joel's. Keep your dirty mind to yourself and keep your grubby paws off him tonight. Of course he's in my room. Where else can I put him? Leslie and Charles are coming tomorrow morning and Gene and Frank get here tomorrow afternoon. Now? Right now he's making us a drink. We're relaxing.

René, love, ever so gently with that vermouth.

He said he'd heard all about the Pines in Paris and London and was dying to see it, and I thought, this is your chance to do a good deed. Aren't you terrible. I've always been interested in good deeds. I introduced you to Walter didn't I? That wasn't my fault.

René model? Of course he's wonderful looking, but God knows what the camera would make of him. What looks good in the bedroom can look ghastly on the page. I can't imagine how he'd look in clothes. Get your mind above your crotch. I mean that I've only seen him in jeans and tee shirts. I tried to make it clear to him that there's something of a premium on looking one's best here. At the very least, one should look interesting. Hold.

The meat goes in the meat keeper. You're a love.

By the way, what does your service charge to drive you out? Mine just went up to one-twenty. Oh, yes, that's with tip. How kind of you to offer, but I really feel I need a car to myself for my sanity. After my week, I'm just not a fit travelling companion. I use the trip to get into my island mood. Hold a second.

René, those things in the blue box should go right into the freezer. No, to the right. There you are.

Here I am. What about Tommy? Why's he staying with you? I thought you didn't like him. Well, my dear, there's a limit to what one should do even for business. Besides, what good is he? I don't think he has it any more. I gave him all of eight pages in the magazine last year. It wasn't less than twenty-four for years. He hasn't made a fashion statement of any significance in ages. Using that ugly lover of his to model his line makes things even worse, if that's possible. I hear his spring line is pure Sixties. Nobody was interested in the Sixties in the Sixties. Well, I'll come for drinks tomorrow, but don't expect me to be my usual charming self if he's there. Five. Five's fine.

René, do you see a pencil over there? Find a pad and write down "Lucas at five" and put a question mark. You may meet him tomorrow. He's dying to meet you. But watch him. Under that dyed hair and lift lurks a ravening beast.

Have you unpacked? You're right. I don't mean to rush you, but you really should. The damp air crawls right inside the bags and makes everything...

Oh, shit! I have to... Do go unpack. This may be my office and God knows how long...

Good grief, is there no such thing as a secret out here? His name is René and he just arrived from France. Why shouldn't he like the island? There aren't many places left in the world that are worth being. Grew up in Marseilles in heaven knows what kind of family. I don't ask rude questions. No, you can't come over for a drink. You'll meet him at dinner later. No, love, not now. You can tell me at dinner what your astrologer said. No. Good-bye. No. Good-bye.

Ah, there you are. Why don't you slip into something beachy. But I should warn you, one doesn't go completely *au natural* at the Pines. That might be the kind of thing they do at the Grove, but the Pines is rather more cosmopolitan. Borrow one of my bathing suits. There's a drawerful in there. If you find one you like, you can keep it.

I swear, every week I come out and look around and try to figure out what in the world Mrs. Higgins does here. I know she's been here, because the check is gone.

Well, I think you look absolutely wonderful in it. We can take a few tucks in it later. My darling, you'd look like Adonis if you were wearing rags.

Come give me a hand. I'll rinse and you tear it into little bite-size pieces. But, my dear, you're French, you're supposed to know all about lettuce. Well, just tear each leaf into small pieces. Cutting it brings out the acid in the leaf. Most people don't understand greens. And then I'll show you how to make the perfect *vinaigrette*.

You're right, *mon cher*, and we'll have lots of time for a little sun. You'll love the simple little supper I've planned. We'll start with the loveliest shrimp bisque that they make up just for me at this funny little restaurant on Madison. They wouldn't give me the recipe, but I told them that if they wanted to keep in my good graces, the least they could do was make it for me every now and then. I gave them a lovely write-up in the magazine. It made them. Tear smaller. I had Mrs. Samuels make *coquilles* and some of her wonderful bread and a *torta di chocolata* to finish.

You saw Mrs. Samuels. She was that little woman who helped Everett get the hampers into the car. She stood right on the steps and waved at us when we drove off.

Smaller, dear.

Are you any good with flowers? I'm sure you're just being modest. Tulips and iris are very easy. Just something casual in that crystal vase over there. I had it made in Venice. I just sketched it for this funny little man and he made it right then and there. I just made him do it over till he got it right.

We're only six for dinner. You'll like most of them. I have no idea where Peter found his lover whatsisname. Peter has a **different one every summer, so it's hardly worth learning their** names. The new one is always high on something or low on something, so I'm never sure where he is when he's here.

My dear, I think it would look ever so much nicer with those dark tulips higher in the center. Roger is in banking, but I have no idea what that means. He's got something or other with him. Greek, I suppose. Well, anyway, dark and swarthy. Phillip and Bruce are... What are Phillip and Bruce? Well, they practically founded the Pines. They say they're responsible for attracting the right people to the Pines, but they never say who.

I don't believe it. You answer it, René. Tell whoever it is I'm swimming. No, they'll never believe it. I'll get it. Tim. Yes, just got here. No, he hasn't. Yes, I suppose. No, can't possibly. Sorry if I sound short, but I'm up to my ears. I think it's very kind of you to have your parents out. It's certainly not what they're used to. Well, I have got used to it. I think bringing them over here is a terrible idea. It's just ducky that they're so understanding, but I don't care to have them understanding me. No, I'm not being touchy and don't call me Jimmy. No one's called me Jimmy in years and you know it. Keep it up and I'll go back to calling you Bubba. No, I never think of "the good old days," and I'll thank you not to. Well, I'm sure you have to run. And by the way, there will be people here tomorrow night who are not likely to find your enchantment with our humble origins in Milwaukee at all amusing, especially me. Oh, go show your mother the meat rack.

Congratulations, René. I can see you tried very hard with those flowers. Just a little touch here and there, and... My heavens, look at the hour. You've finished unpacking us? Aren't you a darling.

No, really I think you look wonderful in my bathing suit. We'll just set the table and go luxuriate on the beach for a bit. You can help. I think the plain Spode this evening. Never dress first night out. I think we should start by touching up the candleabra. You'll find polish under the sink. It's pink with a silver label. I'll get out the silver and crystal. My friends kid me about having fine things at the island, but I tell them that I can't think of any reason for living with less than I enjoy in the city.

Dear, dear, dear! If it's not the phone, it's the door. Who am I expecting? The boy with the liquor. Darling little fellow. Just take the box from him and sign. Put down a five dollar tip. Well, you just write "Tip $5."

No, dear, you have to go all the way out to the outer gate. The lock turns left. No deliveries past the gate. I don't think it does for some people to know what I have here. Hurry back and we'll finish the table in a jiffy and go down for some of that marvelous sun.

Hello! Who is it? Well, I am cross. This phone hasn't stopped since I got here. What can I do for you, Roger? Well, I'm sorry Stavros didn't come. Who are Luke and Sam? Sound like something out of Zane Grey. Well, it's only a modest supper, and I'm not sure it will stretch to seven. I don't do the kinds of things one can just add more potatoes to. I know you wouldn't ask if it weren't important. Yes, I'm sure you are. What are they like? I mean, do you think theyll fit in? You have been known to have exotic tastes in people. That Mischa person, for one. Oh, very well. Of course it will be all right. Don't pay any attention to me, I'm just a little nervy. There's still so much to do and my guest insists on going down to the beach. Let me go. Yes. Yes.

René! René! Now where has he got to? How long does it take to sign a bill and bring back a box? René! God, as if I didn't have enough on my mind. René!

Now where in God's name could he go dressed in a bathing suit? RENE!

PACKING TURTLES
ARNOLD

That box is for books and that one's for shoes and that one's for... What is that one for? Must be for something. I should put labels on them. Well, put what you want in it, Lou. Put any old shit you want in it. I don't care. Let them sort it out.

Wait! I know what that box is for; it's for his turtles. Do you know what it's like to live for six years surrounded by all those goddamned turtles? Everywhere you look there's a turtle staring back. You take cigarettes out of turtles. The Kleenex is in a turtle. Turtle boxes and turtle ashtrays. Glass turtles, marble turtles, crystal turtles. I sit on the john and look at turtle wallpaper. He spent most of last year looking for a turtle telephone. Found one. It's like *The Birds*, only with turtles.

And that Seagram's box is for his clothes. So's that one—that big one. He won't let me give his old clothes away. They don't fit him anymore. He's getting fat. I told him that was dangerous at thirty-five. It's harder to get off after thirty-five. I've kept my weight down. I told him, Go to the gym, like me. He really doesn't care about anything; not even himself.

Jesus, just look at all this stuff.

Oh, Lou, I'm so grateful to you for helping. I don't think I could do this without you.

Tape for the boxes? Under the sink.

How the hell did I get stuck with packing his shit while he's off in St. Croix with that aging twinky he's taken up with? I'm a fool, Lou. You're very sweet and kind to spend your afternoon helping some goddamned old fool who still can't say no to the fat bastard. I'm...

No, the shirts stay on the bed until I can get more boxes. I don't want them to get wrinkled.

Where did you find that? It *belongs* under the sink. Peter and I bought that in St. Thomas on our first vacation together. Awful, isn't it? Why would anyone buy a bottle shaped like a clown full of blackberry brandy? Is it empty? I wonder who drank it? I think we bought it for poor George. George liked blackberry brandy. George liked too much blackberry brandy. Imagine becoming an alcoholic on blackberry brandy. I hated going to his apartment. He slopped it over everything and everything in the place stuck to everything else. Even the cat was sticky. I think Peter thought that bottle was classy. A drunken glass clown: That says a lot about Peter. Oh, just throw the damned thing in the trash.

I really should put labels on the boxes. Well, fuck it, let him and Little Donny sort it out. Let Little Donny start to find out what it's like living with him. Little Donny can unpack and play maid while sweet old Peter sits on his ass in front of the TV. Wait till Little Donny gets a full-time view of the pleasures of Peter. Little Donny will get to do all the shopping and all the cooking and all the cleaning. And if he's real good, he'll get to balance Peter's checkbook and shop for Peter's clothes and stand in line for Peter's theatre tickets.

Peter serves Donny right. Just wait till he starts yelling at Little Donny about not having any clean underwear. And I'll tell you, his underwear isn't all that easy to get clean.

And wait till Big Mama visits. Hah! Big Mama likes to run things and she's always improving things. She carpeted our bathroom in cheap lime-green nylon one year, When you stepped on it, every hair on your body stood on end. Last year she brought us an upholstered pink toilet seat that sticks to you like a leach. That picture of the weeping clown holding the crippled child? From her. "Real oil on real canvas," she said. It's Peter's favorite.

No, Lou; books in that box, shoes in that.

I am going nuts, aren't I, Lou? Tell me to sit down. Tell me to have a drink. I haven't stopped babbling since you got here. Why the hell should you help me clean up my mess? Tell me, Lou, why? Tell me why I ever took up with Peter? I'm a masochist, that's why. I'm my mother all over again with my big, dumb-ass father. I do what she did. She should have set fire to my old man's Barcolounger years ago.

If no more will fit in there, throw the rest out. He'll never notice. He'll be so deliriously happy with Little Donny in their little love nest sucking on Donny's little dong he won't need clothes.

You answer that, Lou. I'm not here, Tell whoever it is you just stopped in to rob the place while I'm in Bellevue.

I don't want to talk to him. I don't care what he wants. I don't care whether he knows I'm here or not.

Hello, Peter. I see you got there in one piece. How's the weather? I see. The packing's going just fine. No, I haven't seen your yellow sweater. I thought you took it with you. Well, I'll look as soon as we get off. Yes, if I find it, I'll take it down to the cleaner on my way to work.

Oh, it's going just fine and Lou's a great help. What bottle? I don't remember it. Well, if I find it I'll wrap it carefully and put it in with your turtles. Of course I'll pack all the turtles...every one of them.

You're not getting too much sun are you? You know you can't take much. Put lots of sunscreen across your shoulders. That's where it's always worse. And don't forget the back of your knees and the tops of your feet.

You went there for dinner. I remember it. Yes, wasn't it? Yes, didn't we?

Well...take good care of yourself. Fine, I'm fine. Yes, I'll see you soon.

Oh, get the fucking bottle out of the trash. No, leave it there. It's finally where it belongs.

You heard me on the phone. Tell me I'm crazy. No, you don't have to. I am crazy. I'm here in New York packing his shit while he's honeymooning with...with that tie salesman.

At least the apartment's mine. Let him build a new nest with the birdbrain. I'm going to redo this place the way I want it. It's about time. He wanted brown walls, we had brown walls. He wanted those nasty slipcovers, we got those nasty slipcovers. And look at that lamp. Just look at that lamp. Will you tell me what it is? What is it? Well, at least it's not a turtle. I'm going to have the whole place painted Kelly green. I want lots of color. This place looks like a faggot funeral parlor.

I am crazy. Why did I tell him I'd take his sweater to the cleaners? Why? You see? I am demented. Anybody in his right mind would have told him to shove his yellow cashmere up his ass. Not me. I'm going to take it to the cleaners. I'm going to be nice. Well, fuck his sweater. Don't wrap those turtles; just throw them in the box. Repairing them will give the lovebirds something to do this winter.

Make us a drink. Make us a strong drink. Have a sandwich. Well, have another one. I'm going to sit here and have a nice strong drink while I unravel his fucking yellow sweater. Then I'm going in and tear down the turtle wallpaper. Go make us a drink.

Soda, please. Soda, if you can find it.

I really should refold those clothes. They'll be a mess by the time he unpacks them.

A PRAYER FOR WHAT?
FRANCIS

There she is again. Always that same awful black dress. I never see her at Mass or taking communion. Why does she come here? Lapsed Catholic? Too cold out? Crazy? It feels colder in here. I should go speak to her. No. If I leave her alone, she'll leave me alone.

She's lighting another candle. That's the third candle she's lit and I still haven't heard any money go into the box. Oh, God, she's turning around. Don't see me. You've lit your candle, lady, why don't you go home and give me a few minutes alone? I just want some peace and I can't even find it in my own church. Light another free candle. Be my guest.

Are you here because you've sinned, lady? Big sins? Little sins? Venial? Mortal? I'm tired of confessing. God, give me some new sins. Give poor Father Gilberti a break. I confess the same things every week, and he gives me the same advice and the same penance. "Bless me, father, for I am about to bore you to death. I have had frequent impure thoughts, had...accidents." What else can I call them?

What must Mrs. Cleary think? We play a game: It didn't happen and she doesn't know and I don't wash my sheets under cover of darkness. I'm the Phantom Laundryman, down in the laundry room at three in the morning, wondering if Father Gilberti can hear that damned old washing machine screaming away. I turn my Walkman up and pretend that old machine won't wake the dead. And I plug in that old iron and pray it won't blow the fuses again or electrocute me.

And how would that saintly old man take hearing
that I take the cross off my wall because I can't keep my eyes
off it? Who sculpted that incredibly beautiful body?
You lied, Father Flynn. In the seminary you said this
passed. "Once you're working eighteen hours a day in some
parish, me boy, you'll go to bed too tired to even think of it,"
says he. "You'll see, me boy, there is no room for impure
thoughts in exhausted minds." Wrong, Father Flynn, there's
room for an army of them in there.
    And when I told him I had "tendencies." "Tendencies?"
says he. "Well—er, ah, em—tendencies, you say? Ah, *those*
tendencies. Well, terrible as they are in the eyes of Christ,
those...tendencies...won't keep you from serving your savior if
you don't act on them. Shower alone, me boy. Shower alone."
The road to salvation is flooded with cold water.
    And the old fraud must have told George the same thing.
"Shower, George, shower." No wonder they said George was
crazy. Water on the brain. But he didn't look crazy when I
found him. He looked exhausted. No, he looked as if he was
pleading with me, as if he wanted me to help him. How could
he do that to himself and then just sit there waiting to bleed to
death?
    I couldn't understand what I was seeing, and now I can't
stop seeing it...over and over. How did he do that much
damage with that dull knife? And that filthy blue rag in his
mouth. Couldn't understand that for days. Of course he bit it to
keep from screaming. Just sitting there on the stones in his
blood and not saying a word, just trying to beat me off, just
trying to get me to leave him the hell alone. Father Shay said it
was God's will that I found him and I should thank God. I
don't. I just don't want George to hate me for stopping him.
What did they do with him? Doesn't matter. Now he's no good
to God or man.

She's lighting another candle and I still didn't hear any money go in the box. I really should speak to her. Oh, to hell with it. Go ahead, light them all, lady. What keeps me here? God help me, I don't give a damn about people. I only half listen to them. I tell them things I only half believe, but they look at me and they hope I do, because if I don't believe, what's left? Oh, yes, my child, there's hope in hopeless situations. There, there. It's God's will. Throw them a little something to keep terrible things from scaring them to death, to keep them from wanting to kill me for being a fraud. Can't be the cause of murderous thoughts in their hearts. That would be leading them into sin.

Confessions are the worst. How do I hear another confession from some poor man who's had sex with another man? "Your immortal soul is in grave danger. Say thirty 'Hail. Marys.'" No, say twenty-nine...we're having a special. How do I tell that man who lives with his lover that he must not touch his Edmund or sleep with him? Every week I tear another piece off him. He asks me why God sent him Edmund to love if it's a mortal sin? It is God's way of testing you and you must cease sinning. I want to tell him to stop coming to me before Edmund gets fed up and leaves him. And wouldn't that be a sin?

But I want to tell all the men to run, even that wretched man who tells me he lusts after little boys. I tell him to honor his marriage. I give him endless rosaries to say, just to keep him busy. Not busy enough. I tell all the married men to avoid the occasions of sin with other men and while I listen I want to know more, to have them whisper every detail through the grill.

And damn that man with the sexy voice. He does tell me everything. He talks so softly that I have to put my ear right against the grill and then I can feel his breath on my ear. He tells me he doesn't want to lose his soul, but he can't give up life, be celibate like me. I tell him to pray, to want a family, to want a woman. I dread his confessions. because I want to know what he looks like. Sometimes I'm sure he's not a penitent, but some man who knows all about me and tells me these awful things because he knows. And when I'm alone, I imagine he confesses to me, because he wants me.

Someday one of them will say, "You don't believe any of this, why should I?"

God! I come here to be alone to think, but I can't stand what I think.

I must stop this. Keep your eye on that woman. Think about what brings her here, keeps her lighting all those candles? They aren't free, lady. But maybe her soul is seeping out of her or she comes here to hide, so IT—that big IT—won't get her. God help me, lady, I should care about you, but I don't.

Well, I can't stay here forever. I'm stiff and it's damned cold in here. Get moving, Francis. Mrs. Cleary will give you hell if you're late for dinner again. And that man's coming for instruction. We both know he's converting to please his fiancee, but I can't just tell him he's a liar, that he doesn't want faith. Oh, and there's that damned ladies' sodality meeting tonight.

I must tell Mrs. Cleary to put more bleach in the wash. The altar cloths look dingy. How long has it been since the brass has been polished or the marble shined? I can even see the dust on the grillwork over the stained glass from here. My God, what kind of world do we live in that forces us to put stained glass in cages? Dear God, where is people's respect for churches? Why in the world should churches have to protect themselves from people?

I COULD STAY
EDDIE

Nice place you got. Like something on TV. You know, when they got some dough. Jesus, you should see the way some of my customers live. You wonder where they get the money for me. I think, Jesus, why don't you beat off and buy yourself a paint job. Real shitholes. But it's a hundred, whether they got a joint or some nice place like this. Aldo tells me I'm too fussy. What's fussy about worrying you get fungus or some scrungy disease just from walking on their floor? I won't even take a drink in some a them. I don't let 'em see I'm rushin' them, but I get 'em down to business and get the hell out.

A hundred don't buy all night, less I like you. Guy up on Fifty-seventh I like. Old guy. Got all this stuff hangin' on 'im. Not fat, you know, just stuff. Big cock. He's prouda that. Takes him awhile to get it up and then he dances around the room waving it. Says he's Glenda the Good Fairy and he's gonna put his wand in me and send me back to Kansas. He's bigger'n Stappy. You seen Stappy. He was next to me at the bar. Got this dick of death. Soft, it's like my arm. But he should get his teeth fixed. He says guys don't buy his face, but I tell him he's not in that dumb Cypress anymore, he's in America. America likes teeth. I got terrific teeth. See.

Why don't we take a bath together or something. I got time. Besides, it's snowing. Not much going on a night like this. Just the old farts out on payday. I made enough tonight, made enough before you.

Look, you want I'll stay over. Same hundred. It's nice here.

But in my business, you can't ask who's got a gold American Express card.

No, that's a joke. I don't take plastic. You think that's funny, but there's lots that do. Pass them at the bar, but they take twenty percent just for handling the paper. You got to look out for the future. I'm putting some away, and I don't mean up my nose.

I see what happens. Herb. You take Herb. Twenty-eight and he's nowhere. He's up Shit Creek, that's where Herb is. Dope. Got a millionaire's habit. Looks like shit...on a bad day. Hasn't got a year left. I told him he'd have a tag on his toe by Easter. But he never liked the business. I do. You meet people.

I learned about meeting people when I ran an elevator in this rich place near the U.N. Got to be real friends with somma the people there. "It's not what you know, it's who you know." My dumb old man didn't know much, but he knew that. Just too dumb and drunk to do anything about it. Come home drunk every night. She'd put him out of bed and he'd get in with me. He'd pretend he was asleep and shove that old cock of his against me and rub. Well, what the hell.

I'm used to drunks. Most of the guys who come to my bar are big drinkers. But they're no trouble. A lot of 'em can't even come in there 'less they're pissed. They get me home and can't do nothing. Had the same guy four times and he didn't remember me one time to another. Just get the money first. They don't like it. "Don't you trust me?" They think we're all crooks. Get to their place and they go hide their money and jewelry. Once, I'm in bed listening to this drunk staggering around trying to figure out where he's going to hide his big fucking treasure. Then he forgets where. I'm in bed next morning and I hear him tearing up his apartment and I know he couldn't remember, so I yelled, "You hid it in the oven, shithead."

Anyway, in this building I was working there was this TV producer. I'd get him going. Had a wife, but I could see he was interested. I'd lean back and pretend my Jockeys were strangling me and shift it around to give him a hint. He'd get all red and his nose would run and he'd hold his hands by his pockets and make these little grabby motions. He said I ever had an idea for a show I should come see him. But he put on those shows about families whose big problem is whether their dumb-ass kid is going to win the basketball game or go to some dance. You know, those shows where nobody ever fucks or goes to the bathroom. But I thought real hard about an idea I could sell him.

He should put on a show about my family. Jesus, then I'd have ideas. He should put on a show about me. I got this guy named Clarence. Gives me two hundred to stay over. He just wants to watch me get myself off, but first I gotta take a bath in this Mr. Bubble stuff. He gives me a bath and dries me off and talks baby talk about how I'm gettin' to be such a big boy. Then I get in these kids pyjamas with the feet in them he gets made. There's this flap in the back. That had me worried at first. He gives me a Teddy Bear to hold while I jack off. Then he tells me I'm a naughty boy and tucks me in. Next morning he runs around the kitchen in a housedress and makes me oatmeal. I figure for two hundred I can eat the shit.

Or Bert. There's a whole series in Bert. I lived with him for two weeks, got to know him like a book. Hot for me, moved me in. He gave me an allowance and let me make what I wanted on the side. Kinky, but I've handled worse. Once I even got away from that crazy bastard that tore that guy's arm off. But with Bert it was all that other crap I couldn't take. He was always after me about the way I talked and ate and what I wore and reading comic books. He wanted to teach me how to

eat. Jesus, I'm twenty-three; I know how to eat. What's
so fucking wonderful about eating with your fork upside down
in the wrong hand?

Course, the real stories you can't put on television. Like
the guys who like it in rubber or leather or dresses. I used to
charge them the same till I learned. They expect to pay more.
It's like the extra dough this actor told me he was getting for
doing something dangerous in this show. But I got this kind of
ESP. I get signals. Worst I ever got was some welts on my ass.
I was new, seventeen, and I got this scary feeling and went
with the guy anyway. You learn in this business.

Are all these pictures real? I mean, not like out of
magazines. You know, if you blindfolded me and got me
someplace and let me look, I could tell you whether I was East
Side or West. Guys on the East got all this stuff on their walls
and all these little empty boxes all over everything. Like that
museum Bert took me to. Guys on the West Side got posters
and the furniture's covered with rugs, like the floor. In the
Village they got all this crazy shit they make themselves.

Your place feels good. It's my ESP. I know I'm OK. I can
relax.

I like you. It's...it's nice. I mean I'll keep the money. You
wouldn't believe what they get for a hotel room, even over
where I live. Even these fucking sneakers are a hundred. One
john, I can get a pair of fucking sneakers. Big fucking deal.

If I could afford it, I'd tell you to have this one on the
house. It's like we're just two guys getting it on.

When you came in, I wondered what a good-looking guy
was doing paying for it. If you had a wife I could understand.

It's nice just laying here. I don't even want a joint. It's
shitty outside and here I am. Fireplace. Christ, you should see
my room.

Yeah, it is late. Sure.

Well, not too late to turn another trick, maybe.

That's OK, I'll get a bath next place or back at the hotel.

Look, I wouldn't take the dough if... We all gotta eat. Gimme your number. I'll give you mine. They can't hire nothin' but drunks to work the desk, so if you call be sure the slob gets the message right. Make him say it back. Make sure he understands. No big deal, but maybe we could get it on again.

YOUR LOVING SON
PHIL

(*Signs letter, then reads aloud.*)
I love you and I still need you. Phil.
(*Reshuffles pages into order and reads.*)

Dear Mom, This is the tenth time I've tried to write this. I hope I can mail this one. I don't want to cut myself off from you and Dad, and I know that if I don't write, that may happen. I don't know what to say to your idea that I've "chosen" to be gay just to hurt you. I don't know how to answer your idea that I'm gay out of spite. I'm just gay and I am as naturally that as grass is green.

You say that I never gave the slightest indication. I can imagine what you mean by that: I seemed normal. As you say, I was such a good boy, got pretty good grades, did fairly well in sports, though never good enough for Dad. I was a good boy, because I didn't want to draw attention to myself. I found out early that if I was quiet and went about my business, I could stay private. Being good was my way of staying secret. And I've always had secrets; especially the secret that I was gay.

I told you the truth, because I felt that I could not go on lying to you about who I really am and to give you the chance to finally know me, with no old lies between us and no new ones that needed telling, like all that stuff I told you about my dating in college or bringing some poor girl like Edith home that Christmas. I think I did her a lot of harm. She was expecting more from me and I've lost her friendship, because I used her.

You hinted in your letter that I waited to tell you I was gay till I'd graduated, so you'd keep on supporting me. The idea makes me angry and ashamed. And, to tell you the truth, I'm not sure it's not true. If that's why I waited, I didn't know it. But does that mean you wouldn't have sent me through school if you had known?

I don't need your money anymore, but I do need you and Dad, need to know that I still have a place with you. It hurts like hell to think that your love for me has always been conditional. My shrink says I have a lot of work to do on that. He says that I have a responsibility for letting things get this tangled and messy. I get furious when he tells me that. I told him that if you and Dad were going to cut me out of your lives, I couldn't see any point in working on my problems with you, because you wouldn't be around. He says that whether I ever see you again or not, my relationship with you will always be there. I hear him and it makes me angry, because I can feel he's right.

You say that if I'd written to tell you I was gravely ill you could handle it better than this. Have you any idea how that makes me feel, knowing that you would rather deal with my having cancer or being in some awful disabling accident? Or crippled? But, of course, you would prefer a grave illness that didn't include AIDS? Dead giveaway, that. As it is, I'm afraid I'm disappointingly well and likely to be happy. My God, Mom, think before you write such things.

You write that you haven't told Dad yet, because if he knew it would kill him. Why is my being gay enough to cause death? He never expected all that much of me anyway. It was you who always told me that no matter how he behaved

towards me he really loved me. He never told me that.
Are you saying that my being gay is a test his unsspoken love
couldn't stand? If you sense some bitterness in what I say,
you're right.

Now to the trip you may still be planning. Glen says he'll
move out while you're here, but I don't want him to. It would
be like Laura's husband moving out when you go there to visit.
If Glen moved out, it would be like telling you that I was
ashamed of him or that we were doing something that needed
hiding. I'm proud of him and who we are. We're nice people.

You also say that you don't know how you could bring
yourself to tell Laura and B.J., because they love me so much.
Maybe they love me because they know. I was twelve when I
told them, and I can still feel my heart hammering away when
I remember trying to work up my nerve to do it. Neither of
them fainted and Laura said she'd guessed and, to quote her,
"So what?" B.J. had some trouble with it, his main concern
being my not taking to wearing dresses or messing around with
his football team. He's still uncomfortable and he tells me so,
but it isn't enough to keep him from caring about his little
brother or promising to beat the hell out of anybody who gives
me trouble.

So, I haven't lost all of you. Maybe Laura and B.J. are the
most family I can have. I know there has to be a price for
demanding to be my own man in my own way. But please,
Mom, think: I'm your son. I'm just not who you thought I was
or who you planned on my being. But you .know me in ways
that no one ever will, so I pray that you'll find a way through
this.

I don't mean to lecture, but I should explain what being
gay means to me, because I don't want you to think that it's
just a matter of sex. Sex is a part of it, but it's just the part that

shows on the outside. Sure, it's all about an affinity for men in every way, but not only in the way most people think. I think God has made a special kind of man and He's given him a way of seeing and using the world that is very different from the way straight men and women see and use it. I think gay people even have special things to do in life. Because of our difference we contribute things that are special, sometimes even beautiful.

Being gay may even make me stronger, because I may have to go through life without a family I can turn to, with a lot of laws stacked against me, with employers who may not judge my work but my sex, even with churches that don't want my kind.

Well, I've said it all and I hope that I'll be able to send this one. A lot of your letter hurt like hell, so my fear is that I won't mail this and I'll just stop writing or calling. I explained to Dr. Szell that staying out of your lives might solve all our problems. He says not, but I'm not sure I believe him. Maybe I should just stay away for a while or wait till you can write me again.

And if you write, please don't close with "yours sincerely" again. Close with "your loving mother" the way you always used to.

I love you and I still need you.

Phil

(*He stares at letter on his lap, picks it up and crushes it.*)

EPICS AREN'T EASY
LUDLOW

Get on the bed again, Bobby, we want to check the lighting. And take those socks off.

Because they're an anachronism. That means that socks didn't exist when our film takes place. And we're all working very hard to make our film very special, not just another piece of cheap...

You must imagine that you're in Caligula's bedroom in ancient Greece and that you've just been bought by the Emperor.

On your stomach, dear. No, just lay there; no acting just yet.

How does he look with the purple gel? Let me see.

(LUDLOW *squats to peer through viewfinder.*)

You're right, it makes his behind look like a couple of Easter eggs. Maybe another lens.

No, we'll stick with the pink gels. Change 'em back, Lucas.

Have you got a full magazine in the camera, Dan?

And where's Clarence?

What, Bobby?

Don't mumble, Bobby.

Why are you two always arguing?

Go get him, Dan. Try the john. That's where he usually sulks.

Lucas, I thought I asked you to fix that rip in the marble pillar. And where's the candleabra?

So what if they didn't have French candleabras in ancient Greece?

If *I* didn't know that, how would the audience?

Jesus, you try to give a movie a little panache, a few production values...

Sit up and let's hear your lines, Bobby. Sit up straight.

They're not slimy, they're silk. Now sit up.

Because sitting up gives your diaphragm support.

No, no, Bobby, it's, "I am but a boy of the hills, sire, stolen and sold like poor peasant pottery, and brought here to be shamed and humiliated as no freeborn man should. I beg your mercy." Then he says, "I am Caligula. What know I of mercy and nor do I care. I care only that my flesh is immoderately pleasured." And you say...

Well, welcome back, Clarence. Now, let's get to work. Out of those clothes. And do put your Mickey Mouse tee shirt out of my sight. It ruins my mood.

Let's try them again, Bobby.

They're perfectly clear. "I am but a boy of the..."

Now what, Clarence?

Well, Bobby is wrong. He is not going to get more closeups than you.

No, not anywhere.

No, not of anything.

Again, dear.

No, Bobby: "I am but a boy of the hills, sire..." Siiii-errrr. Not "sir." You're not his butler.

Wristwatch, too, Clarence. Sit next to Bobby.

Now, we're all here in ancient Greece. You, Bobby, have been brought to Caligula's bedroom to give him pleasure.

What? No, I don't think you should dance for him first, Bobby.

Well, I didn't ask you to make up a dance.

Yvonne deCarlo probably did.

Now, let's run our lines before we shoot. We'll start with the two-shot, Dan. Bobby, you look to the right of the lens as you speak. You look anguished.

No, I don't think he'd cry. Clarence, you play with his hair and look at him lasciviously.

Lasci...You're hot for him.

Give Lucas your gum, Bobby.

He'll take very good care of it. Now, "I am but a boy of the hills, sire."

It means you grew up on a farm. You raised sheep. You know all about sheep.

Oh, Christ. Just say, "I don't know what you want of me, sire."

Yes, that's all.

Well, you're not getting a closeup if you don't know your lines.

Again. "I don't know what you want of me, sire."

You may know what he wants, but this innocent boy from the hills doesn't. Well, pretend you don't. That's what people do in movies; they pretend.

Now! "What do you want?"

Play with his hair, Kip. His *hair*. Because Bobby is having trouble with his lines and what you're doing distracts him.

No, Bobby, not "Whatcha want, sire?" "What do you want?" and forget the fucking sire.

Yes, that was a very good try, Bobby. But let's simplify the scene. Just roll over, Bobby. Yes, I know they're slippery.

Let go of his hair, Clarence. And, please, stop looking lascivious. Well, just look interested. Pretend this is the hottest hunk you've seen since that gladiator.

A gladiator is...

Are they still in frame, Dan? Oh, Christ, of course I see it.
Why did you have to pick last night to do it, Clarence?
Why?

Well, Dan, we'll just have to pretend that butterfly tattoos
were common in ancient Greece.

Quiet!

Roll 'em!

(*Blackout simultaneous with* BOBBY*'s voice braying loudly,*
"Whatcha want, sire?")

THREE MEN AT THE EDGE
TOBY, HANK AND LEONARD

TOBY: For me it was candy.

HANK: For me it was Christmas.

LEONARD: For me it was soap.

TOBY: I didn't feel a thing.

HANK: Just tired.

LEONARD: Out of it.

TOBY: Of course there was the mark.

HANK: Purple.

LEONARD: A bruise.

TOBY: I thought so too.

HANK: Small as a shirt button.

LEONARD: Didn't hurt.

TOBY: I was the fourth of my friends.

HANK: I felt alone.

LEONARD: I had Bill.

TOBY: I denied it. I'd just bumped into something.

HANK: I ignored it.

LEONARD: I should have.

TOBY: Do you know what it's like to have your doctor put up his hands and back away from you as if you were a vampire?

HANK: They told me what case number I was...as if I'd gotten in some marathon.

LEONARD: I told my doctor that if he didn't use drugs and stayed out of backroom bars, he was probably safe, because I had no intention of kissing him...no matter how much he begged.

TOBY: I told Chris and he told Terry...and Carmine...and Howard. And he told... Oh, what difference does it make?

HANK: Earning a living! That's what difference.

LEONARD: Bullshit! Seeing next year or even next week...that's what difference.

TOBY: I found a support group. We trade war stories. We call one another at weird hours with weird thoughts.

HANK: My work-week is only three days. Barely make that.

LEONARD: I got out of my showcase. Told them I was doing a bus-and-truck of *Elephant Man*. Now why did I pick that show? I suppose that's what I felt like. I played Hamlet in college. I was already planning my Lear.

TOBY: You tell people and their head does this funny click to one side, as if they'd been slapped.

HANK: They look around for exits.

LEONARD: So do I.

TOBY: Some run.

HANK: Some stay.

LEONARD: I don't blame Bill. I just hate him sometimes. I hate health. All his black hair and clear skin. Why the fuck did I take up with a model? It's like being in some show where the only other actor has all the good lines. I should have taken up with Fred. Even half-dead I look better than Fred.

TOBY: Thank God, I've got a gay boss. I'm a good programmer. He's keeping me on. He told me not to tell anyone. He was right.

HANK: My doctor, called my company and said I had a low-grade fever and would have to work short weeks.

LEONARD: I finally told Bill. God, but he was wonderful. He didn't even suggest that I wear a bell around my neck. He was so understanding, so gentle and thoughtful...and it just enraged me. I wanted him to have it and I wanted to be understanding. I wanted to kill him. He's lucky I didn't when he came up with that shitty business about the soap.

TOBY: For me it was candy.

HANK: For me it was Christmas.

LEONARD: Soap, for Christ's sake, soap! Did I think that...would it be all right if...would I mind terribly if...? Course, Bill, honey baby mine. Sho 'nuff, we can use separate bars of soap. We can have separate soap dishes and I'll dry with paper towels we can burn and eat off paper plates we can throw out and shave off my hair so I don't have to use the goddamned comb. Oh, shit!

TOBY: Lolly gave me the candy. Happy birthday. They kidded me about being twenty-nine. Nobody's twenty-nine. You know offices...anything to break the routine. Two whole pounds of Fannie Farmer creams. And lots of cards. I can't stay away from candy and I have this weight thing. Can you believe I'm still worried about gaining weight. I took them into my boss and held them out, but he just sat there looking at my hands and I didn't understrand. I said, My hands are clean, and he said, No, it's... I shouldn't have cried.

HANK: My parents were so beautiful about my being gay. They said they loved me as I was. No conditions, no ifs, ands, or buts. Just as I was. Hi, Mom, it's Hank. Mom, I've got pretty bad news. She cried and said she'd call back. Four days. Four days it took. We love you, but don't come home for Christmas. Well, no, not Thanksgiving either. Look, child of my own, life of my loins, just stay away. There are others to think of—your brothers and their wives and their children. I suppose they burn the letters I send. I can't call. I guess it's all said.

LEONARD: Bill's going away on business for four days. That's too long these days.

TOBY: My boss is one of those don-t-give-up-the-ship types. There's always hope. Tomorrow is another day. Who says?

HANK: I don't think I want to wait it out. I don't think I can.

LEONARD: Well, at least nobody's had the bad taste to send me a get-well card.

TOBY: Don't give up the ship.

HANK: Don't come home for Christmas.

LEONARD: And, for Christ's sake, don't use the soap.

THE PERILS OF PRINT
CHRIS

...twelve, thirteen, fourteen.

Fourteen lines times eight dollars a line is...is a hundred and thirty-two dollars! My God! For one ad? Who's out there who's worth that?

And who reads these things?

I do, but who else?

And who answers these things?

I know what Howard got when he ran his: He got that guy from *Nightmare on Elm Street*. Strange things are lurking out there.

I could fly to Key West for less. I could buy five good porno tapes. I could go to forty bars and have two beers in each.

And how am I supposed to get all those letters in those little boxes? What if I spell something wrong? How do you change it? You don't. Wanted: Hunky *Spud*. I'd get Mr. Potato.

And is there a hundred thirty-two left on my MasterCard?

Maybe I can cut it.

(Reads.)

Please read this:

I know these ads are supposed to sound exciting or sexy or glamorous or a little dangerous—or even a lot dangerous—but I thought I'd try telling the truth. The truth is that I just don't like being alone, or getting older alone, or living with only the sound of my own voice, or sleeping in a bed that seems to get bigger every year. My looks are passable. Some people think

I'm wonderful in bed, some think I'm awful. On our first date I'll try not to make you think I have it all together, that I have tons of friends, and go to marvelous places all over the world, all the time. I'm not sensational, but I might do nicely. I'm exhausted by being terrific. I'd just like to be with someone.

Chris.

Great! Theyll think my mother wrote it. "I got this nice clean kid. Hardly used."

Who'd want somebody like that?

MEMORIAL ARMOIRE
BRENDAN

Lawrence? Brendan. I thought you should...
Of course I know what time it is.
Old people don't need as much sleep.
Does your doctor know how much you're sleeping at your age?
Sorry to wake Sleeping Beauty, but I thought you'd want to know...
What noise? Oh, it's ice. I'm having a drink.
I'm old enough to drink when I want. Yes, at 2 a.m. What has age got to do with drinking?
Besides, I'm having a drink because I can't sleep, and I thought you'd want to know that Donny died an hour ago. No one will ever convince me that hospitals aren't dangerous.
They didn't do Donny any good.
It's as well. It was only going to get worse. He sounded just like a short wave radio tonight...kept fading in and out. HELLO BRENDAN...h o w a r e y o u...i-m—j-u-s-t—f-i-n-e ...I'M O.K.
Your phone's fine: I was imitating Donny fading.
What? What in the world makes you think he's in Heaven? Did he say he wanted to go there? Well, even if he said he wanted to go there doesn't mean he'll get there. He never told me that. He always told me he hoped that wherever he went they'd show a lot of movies. No, I don't think he meant to be funny. He was never funny. Oh, he'd say funny things, but I never thought it was intentional.

When did he get interested in Heaven? He always said Heaven looked awful in paintings; all that heavy drag and sitting around staring up at doves. He said no sane person stood under doves and stared up.

I know the pictures are allegorical, but why should saints be any safer? Are you always this grumpy when you wake up?

Why does Donny make you think of Tully? They're both dead, but there the resemblence ends. I still wonder what happened to Tully's Tony Award. It was always on his mantle.

What an awful thing to remember. Imagine Tully being too proud to use a bed pan and crawling into the bathroom. Didn't make it though. Shot a turd clear across the room.

Oh, him. Hank was always a hypochondriac. The least little thing. Tried to get his doctor to hospitalize him for crabs. Died anyway.

No, not of crabs. Oh, go back to bed.

Well, I'm sorry you're wide awake, but I thought you'd want to know about Donny.

I know he was seventy-nine, but I've called him Donny for fifty years.

How many of us are there left?

That's more than I would have thought. Who is there?

Oh, he doesn't count. He's only sixty-two. I mean of our crowd.

With Donny gone, I count five.

How did I forget Henry? I'm always forgetting Henry. Make it six, at the most.

When I saw Donny tonight, I could barely see his poor little face on the pillow...white on white, like those terrible shirts he wore.

He wasn't himself though. He was always so dignified when he was well. Tonight he lay there with those things up his nose and went on and on about sex. Said the medication they gave him made him horny. Horny at seventynine. Said he had an erection all the time. I'm glad I didn't see it. I told him he couldn't tell the difference between passion and arthritis. All he did was talk about sex, so don't tell me he wanted to go to Heaven. He kept insisting I knew some old lover of his named Karl. Do you remember a Karl? Said Karl had the most beautifully proportioned piece of meat he'd ever seen. And there was a Norman. Enormous Norman. All these years and I never knew that side of him.

The old fool even said the male nurse was after him...something about bathing him suggestively. He said it was the pills they were giving him.

They're orange and pink. Why?

He wanted to give me some.

Of course I didn't take them. How do I know what they're called?

They certainly got the old crock going. All this nonsense about sex. Something about some hall porter at his hotel in Vienna who seduced him in the elevator and a steward on an airplane and a porter on a train. Sex everywhere but in an ox-cart. And when it wasn't on some plane or train it was in some country...Munich, Florence, Singapore. He always talked about how hard he worked on those trips. Tonight he went on and on...like Bernadette describing what happened at Lourdes.

No, I didn't stay long. I couldn't stand hearing all that foolishness. Truthfully, it wasn't the sex so much as that awful farting.

No, you old fool, not me, *him.* It made this strange floppy noise and the most dreadful... And all he's been eating is bland food and Jello. But it seemed to cheer him up. Not the food, the farting. He said it showed there was life in the old boy yet. I said it smelled more like something died.

I didn't mean to be tactless. I've been home for hours. Came right home and got to work updating my obituary. I always keep it up to date. There's always something new to add. I'm still getting awards and honoraries. Oh, I know they're looking to be remembered in my will. So what? Doesn't mean I don't deserve the awards. They look nice on the walls. All 32 are out being reframed. Going to cost me over $2000.

I always write my own obituaries; friends never get them right. It's too emotional a time for them. I send it over to the *Times* for their files. Lots of people do. I have earned a certain distinction and I don't want some hack making me sound like a nonentity.

I'll call in Donny's obituary and let you know what your share is.

It's expensive. I think it would be a nice gesture if his old friends shared the expense.

So sad. Well, if nothing else, I'll have the armoire to remember him by.

The one in the living room. It was the only one he had. Oh, no, you must be wrong, he said it would come to me. When did he tell you that?

You must have misunderstood.

I know your hearing's fine. So is mine. Besides, Donny and I were always close. I found him his first apartment, gave him his first Cuisinart. We'll just have to wait for the will, won't we? So, there's no sense talking about it.

I don't sound irritated, because I don't feel irritated.

Well, I won't keep you from your beauty sleep. Besides, I want to freshen my drink.

No, I'm not drinking too much for my age. And speaking of age, I'm seventy-three...two whole years younger than you. And where in the world would you fit an armoire in all that stuff?

We'll just have to wait for the will, won't we?

Goodnight.

I'm fine. Just fine. I just thought you'd like to know that Donny left us or passed on...or we lost him or whatever the hell happened.

Goodnight.

I'm fine.

Goodnight.

I am just fine.

No.

Goodnight,

(*Hangs up.*)

Damn you, Donny.

WE'LL BE EIGHTY-FIVE
DANA

I think Mr. Farringer will love the way it looks, Geoffrey. You're sure you've got enough food? Mr. Farringer hates running out. He says it looks chintzy. Be sure and tell your new bartender to make the first drink strong and then ease up, unless they ask for strong ones, of course. Mr. Page always does and we have to lay him out under the piano. I've kept that table clear for birthday presents. Do you think there are too many flowers in the living room? Have those roses on the breakfront put in the bedroom. No, the Rossiters sent them. Take the gardenia plant into the bedroom. And do tell the kitchen people to be very careful with the china. We're using the antique Havilland tonight. Bring me your bill before you leave and I'll give you a check. Oh, and have someone bring me a very light scotch and water. I'm going to be stuck here.

I'll get the door. Oh, and remember the gardenia plant.

Am I glad to see you. Give me that while you hang your coat up. It's a book. Which? He'll like that, especially if it's not out yet. He must have every book on Canaletto ever published.

Ah, thank you, Geoffrey. And would you mind bringing Mr. Tippet a drink? What will you have, Roger?

Carroll's birthdays wear me out. He says he'd settle for one every three years, but people do remember. In his business it's sheer spite.

(*Phone rings.*)

Oh, shit. Go find your drink. Bar's in the library tonight.

Lewis? Oh, don't worry about that. There are going
to be eighty-five of us. Of course it's not sit-down. It's the
usual Carroll Farringer birthday mob-scene? Well, you should
know about television's elite. Well, hurry your engineer up and
get here when you can.
Lewis will be late. I wish everybody would be late.
Everything's ready, but I always feel it's not. It's one of
Carroll's brand-name nights and he gets to write the whole
thing off on his taxes.
Jesus! that can't be the first guests...and twenty minutes
early, damn them. They'll just have to fend for themselves.
George! Hannah! No coats! I thought you gave the car up
and Simon went with the Becks. You're right: New York's
impossible without one. We're putting the gifts on the empty
table in the living room. He'll love it. Where in the world did
you find a second one? Carroll's been looking for one for
years. Well, just make yourselves comfortable and get a drink.
Carroll should be out in a few minutes. Oh, excuse me, you
know Roger Tippet. I think you met at the Guild party.

Carroll wants another Lalique decanter like he wants
another head in his hole. Well, he'll pretend it's just the
greatest thing he's got since Mommy's tit. He should be acting
in his series, rather than producing them.

Well, only eighty-three to go. God, when I think that all I
wanted in New Mexico was to come to New York and meet
famous people. Be careful what you pray for. They need a lot
more attention than the average human. Carroll's terrific at it.
That's why he's so successful, I suppose.

I do wish Carroll would manage to get ready on time. If I
left things to the last minute he'd... Well, he depends on me
and I... No, I don't mind. God knows, he does enough for me.
Besides, after nine years you get used to... All this gives me
something to...

Ah, more guests or more flowers or more something.

Leon! Chris! Give me your coats. Well, the last I saw of Carroll he was getting into the shower. He'll make a late and very dramatic entrance. Gifts go on the table in there. What? Course, it's no trouble. If Tally calls you've gone to a screening and he's not to wait for you at L'Entrecote. No, I'll be happy to. Talbot, screening, no L'Entrecote.

Oh, I don't think they mean anything by it; it's just their way. They treat everybody like the hired help. I'm used to them by now. I am supposed to be Carroll's secretary. Well, that, too. You know as well as I do it's the best way to manage this kind of thing. You can't go waving it in people's faces. Diana's Carroll's date tonight. Well, he can't have me hanging on his arm.

He just can't, that's why.

Don't tell me what old friends are for. I know what they're for. Carroll's not forcing me to do anything. We've worked out a very good...

Damned phone. Hello! Oh, don't worry about it, just tell Martha to take good care of herself. There must be some doctor who'll come. Walter might. I'll give you his number. Seven-five-five, three-four-oh-two. I'll tell Carroll. Oh, don't bother sending Henry over with the present. He'll be half the night opening what's here. He'll just be sorry you can't make it. No apology needed, just take care of Martha.

She's ill. She gets everything. She's probably pregnant again.

Do you think all those flowers make the living room look like a wake? I suppose they do.

When did I tell you that? I don't remember. Well, we'd obviously both had too much to drink. I don't need you to worry about me. Carroll didn't mean it. We'd both had a rotten day and we took it out on one another. I wasn't all that scared. If I said that, I was exaggerating. I was probably too drunk to hurt. Feeling no pain. Well, I'm sorry I called you over a family spat. That's all it was, a spat. OK, a fight. But, for Christ's sake, my life wasn't in danger. If I said that, I was really drunk. It doesn't happen all the time. Just leave it.

Where would I go? You going to take me in?

Yeah, I know you would.

Where is everybody? That elevator can only take six at a time. We'll be all night getting them up here.

Listen, love, New York doesn't need another actor, and an aging one at that. It's up to it's ass in actors and that one bus-and-truck knocked the shit out of a lot of my illusions. That's over...and thank God.

Two years with Herbert Berghof doesn't prepare one for much, except starvation.

Leave it, Roger. Go get yourself another drink.

Well, if you don't want another drink, I do. A strong one.

Why is it that every bell in the place always goes off at once?

Charlie! Leora! Be dears and hang them up while I get the phone. You know Roger. Hello! No, I'm sorry they're not here. They couldn't. Well, his client insisted they meet him at a screening...something about a rough cut coming in from the coast. No, they didn't say where, but I was to tell you they won't be able to meet you at the restaurant. Yes, well I wish I could be more helpful. Well, I'm sorry, but I'm only delivering their message. I think you'll have to tell them that yourself.

That's a beautiful dress, Leora. The presents go in the living room.

Roger, be a love and get me that drink.

For God's sake, what are you doing out here in your robe? Only six, so far. It's still early. They all accepted. It's not my fault. Of course the invitations said seven; I showed them to you. You said you wanted ham. There's plenty of other things to eat. I can't think of... Of course I'm supposed to, but... Why aren't you dressed? Well, I didn't take them. No, I didn't borrow them. Why does it have to be those links? Look in the bathroom. You take them out and put them in the medicine chest now and then.

Yes, I remembered Loomis. And Edgar. Yes, I'll tell him to bring you a martini in the bathroom. It's too early for a double. I know it's your birthday. Now get out of sight. Do you want the guests to see you? Yes, I'll stay here. Make up your mind. I can't be in two places at once. What about Claire? No, you didn't mention her. I'm sure you didn't. Well, if you did I don't remember and I'm sorry. I can't... Yes, I should. If I did, I'm sorry. If there was something I could do to make it right I would. I said I'm sorry. Yes, I'll remember your drink. Right away. Yes, immediately.

Leave it, Roger. He doesn't mean to sound so... He's always edgy before a big party. Yeah, before a little party, too.

Oh, Roger, be a good friend and shut up. Because he's right. I shouldn't have forgotten.

Well, isn't that just dandy for you. You can hack it, deal with those grubby people, get an agent, go without. I tried it and it made me feel...

I earn my keep. I can do this. This is what I know how to do. It suits me.

Shit, Roger! Your line should be delivered by someone sitting on a white horse and wearing silver armor. What the fuck about the future? What future?

LATE

RICHARD

You don't have to tell me I'm late, Helen. If you want to complain, call the goddamned railroad.

I'm in a shitty mood, because it's been a shitty day. So, don't make it a shitty night.

I can't yet.

Then feed the kids and let them get to their game.

Then I'll eat it dried out.

Because I have to call the office.

Because it's what pays for everything.

No, I don't know how long I'll be.

Do that.

(*Punches out number on phone and sits.*)

Sam, it's Richard. Yes, finally.

What a day. Rita's out sick, Bloom had a bug up his ass, forty-eight pages of mechanicals sized wrong, page proofs late, I have to drive to Cherry Hill Sunday night.

You were smart to leave, Sam. Christ, if I could afford it...

I'm sorry I haven't been able to return your calls.

Last Wednesday? I couldn't have made a date for Wednesday. It was Nick's birthday and Helen would have had my...

You know I wouldn't do that intentionally. I get busy and...God, you should know me by now.

I'm sorry. I really am. You know I...

Oh, Sam, please say something nice. I need a little consideration. I feel raw.

Look, just leave it. I'll make up for Wednesday.

You needed to do what in person?

Wait a minute.

Don't say a word, Nick. I recognize your urchin look. Ten enough? I suppose Chrissy needs some too. Why doesn't Chrissy ask for his own money?

Yeah, you are better at it?

Have fun.

Now... Let's make it Monday. No, not Monday. Tuesday. Drinks at the Bull and Bear and, if I can, I'll stay over.

It can't be a month.

I think of you all...

All right, get a word in.

Florida? Does that mean no Tuesday? If it's been a whole month since, I'd think you...

It has to be more than twenty-three times in two years.

How can you keep books on us? I'm with you as often as I can be.

I've told you how I feel.

Then you haven't been listening.

Why does it all have to be said?

Because I don't say those kinds of things, I don't make those kinds of promises.

It's more than I've ever felt for anyone.

Running to Florida's childish.

What you mean is that if you can't have all of me you're...

What is it, Helen?

I'll eat it cold.

Something else?

Then don't hover.

Because I'd sooner you didn't, godammit.

Then here! You take the phone. You get this fucking mess

settled and I'll go eat the fucking roast.
Why now?
My God, you owe me something. Are you just going to walk off as if I didn't mean shit. Christ, you can wait a day, spare me an hour.
I haven't done anything.
It hasn't been easy on me either.
Because you don't have any other obligations.
Wait till tomorrow. I'll tell Helen I have an emergency in the office and come in.
Of course I'd try to talk you out of it.
How much can I say on the phone? There are two extensions.
You really don't know what this is doing to me, do you? This is all about you, about what you need, what you want. What about me and what I need?
Wait! What is it, Chrissy?
Leave it on the kitchen table and I'll see if I can fix it.
Because Daddy's busy.
You have a good time. And stay near Nick.
You had everything I had to give.
Well, fuck you, if it wasn't enough. It's all I had. Everybody's taking a piece of me and there's not much left.
Oh, Sam, please. give me your flight number.
Please. When? Out of where? Please.
(*Writes.*) American. Nine-fifteen.
Oh, Jesus, Sam. How could I? Not in a crowd.
I'll write.
No! Don't write me here. And not the office. Care of Frank.
Sam? You there?
(*The phone is dead. He puts it down.*)

What the hell now, Helen?

It's waited this long, it can fucking well wait while I have a drink. It's the fucking office. What else would it be? Would it be asking too goddamned fucking much for you to make me a drink?

ONE MORE WINDBAG
DES

(*Waiting offstage to be announced on a television talkshow.*)
Jesus! Twenty-three interviews in six days. Well, prove you're an actor, pretend you like this old gasbag, that you want to be on his silly-ass show.
Well, here I go, hot on the heels of Fix-o-Dent, Preparation H, and Summer's Eve.
(*Matches following with actions.*)
Head up, lock the smile on, walk briskly, smile at the audience, smile at Huey, shake his greasy paw, hold for applause, look humble, sit.

It's wonderful to be back on your show, Huey, and it's very kind of you to ask me. I missed seeing your show when I was on location. It's been a favorite of mine for years.

Lay it on thick. I'd almost sooner be back waiting tables. Well, almost.

I always find that question odd, Huey, because I sure as hell don't feel like a sex symbol.

I'm so much meat on the hoof. The minute the love handles slop over my belt I'll sign for a television series and go on as long as I can. It's all I know how to do.

Wouldn't you be flattered if so many women fussed over you?

How would you like middle-age ladies edging up to you and brushing their tits against you. They want to go back to Dubuque and tell Aunt Maude they got within smelling distance of me and I'm so much shorter than I look in movies. Damned near a midget, Maude. That dame in the first row's staring at my crotch as if she's guessing how many beans are in the jar.

Oh, sure I miss being a private person, going shopping or just out to dinner with a woman, but I know how lucky I am to have my career, to have fans tell me I've touched their lives, given them pleasure.

What I ache to do is be with Ben. Any damned place, doing any damned thing.

Oh, the papers are always reporting problems on location, Huey, but when you see *A Sea of Evils* I think you'll agree that we've turned out a terrific movie.

A Sea of Evils is a swamp of boredom. The director was always coked to the eyes. All he was shooting was blanks. Well, not my first rotten movie. My problem was three months away from Ben in that Phillipine hell-hole. Three months of virginity, except for long-distance masturbation. Sex with anything local would only get me several pages in a medical journal.

Working with Denise was a wonderful experience. She's new to the business, but she's a real pro and she's going to be a big star.

She'll be a big waitress again, as soon as the producer stops schtumping her. What a bitch. Tells Harry she won't kiss me, because she knows where my mouth has been. I told her the idea of kissing someone who'd been swinging on the producer's withered organ didn't fill me with delight. What's he asking me? Oh, yes.

My divorce was hard. I'm basically a family man and I thought that now that my career seemed solid, I could start having a family with Sheila. Sad for us.

The divorce was the only thing that was hard. But she
got fifty thou for four months as my wife and two parts at
Universal. Sheila didn't have to shag ass through ten years of
summer stock or wait tables. Now what? Pay attention, Des.
Pay attention.
     I'd love to have children. But kids need time and love and
parents who can help them grow into solid adults.
I'd also love pellagra and a pet python. What's he saying? I
really must concentrate. Ah, so he's finally gotten around to it.
Keep it light.
     Oh, well, you know the *National Enquirer*. But I won't sue
them for slander. My old buddy Ben moved in when both
our marriages fell apart at the same time. We helped one
another through. We've been friends since we played
football at Northwestern.
He made my career possible. All because of him, while I was
just background in commercials or an extra in a mob. Payed
for my lessons, got my ass out the door for rounds. What about
Valerie? Valerie who? Oh!
     Well, Valerie and I do share a lot. We love the same sports,
music, have the same sense of humor. We go way back to...
Babble on. Give 'em what they want. As if their admission
ticket bought them a peek into my bedroom.
     I'm sorry, Phil...sorry, *Huey*. What did you ask? My next
film starts shooting in...
Why don't I just tell 'em what they really want to know? No,
ladies, I'm not sensational in bed and there's not one of you
who wouldn't find me a big fat disappointment.
     Sorry, I'm wandering. Jet lag I guess.
Oh, shit, you silly bugger, cut to your Alpo commercial and let
me get home to Ben. You bore me. I bore me. I'm tired. I'm
tired of telling lies and I miss Ben and...

And you ask the silliest dumb-ass questions I've heard on this whole fucking cockamamie tour.

Now why did the audience gasp?

Oh!

THREE MEN AT A BAR

NICK, TREVOR AND CORY

NICK: (*Looking in mirror.*)
I've tried on everything I own and I still look like hell. The haircut's awful. I'm getting a zit. I've got the wrong head on the wrong body.
I don't care.
If Mr. Muscles's there tonight, I'll go right up to him. "Hi, my name's Nick. I..." I what? "I work at Saks in mens' socks. You know...knee-high, over-the-calf." That'll get him all excited. "I was born in Detroit." Another thriller.
You can't get near him anyway. All those friends of his. Always in that corner in a huddle. Probably friends from some gym. Eight hundred muscles...on five men. I'd get him home, he'd put his arms around me and break something. Crunch! Big night in the emergency room. Romance in traction.
I should change my type. I should change my type to something I stand a chance of getting.
Not me.
TREVOR: (*Looking in mirror.*)
Only ten? It was ten an hour ago.
Why doesn't anybody go out before eleven on Friday.
This tie is all wrong with this suit, but who'll notice in The Black Hole?
Why do I bother? The place hasn't changed in seven years. Same dusty saddles hanging all over the place, same fake corrals. All I've ever hauled out of there is eight guys who were all named Whatsisname.

It's all so tediously predictable. At eleven-thirty those bikers in leather come storming in, have one beer, look us over like a penful of pigs at the state fair and stalk out, as if we've offended them by not being gorgeous. At twelve, Henry's bleached head will hit the bar and Chris will ask him to leave. At one, that demented old fart who dresses like some rock star will get desperate and ask everybody whose too drunk to run to go home with him. At two I intend to be much too drunk to care.

CORY: (*Looking in mirror, adjusting his hair, sniffing.*)

It's the glue. That's what I smell.

I should have gotten the "Front-Line Executive", instead of the "Mediterranean Maestro". The "Executive" didn't look so...so *young*. I look nineteen. From the eyebrows up.

(*He walks stiffly about.*)

The salesman said I could swim in it. I can barely walk in it.

Must be careful how much I drink with this, until I know what it's going to do.

Oh, God, why did I do it? I feel like I'm wearing a Pekinese.

Christ, but I've gotten expensive. Thousands for caps. Thousands for the tucks. Hundreds for a gym. All to keep the old ruin in shape. I feel like Williamsberg.

It's hateful. My elbows look like old apples. Even my earlobes have wrinkles.

(*Lights down, then up immediately.*)

NICK: It's too damned dark in here. He'll never see me over here.

Here! Now he can see me when he looks in the mirror. But what if he doesn't look that way?

Here! There's good light every time they open the door.

Smells rotten here. Too near the john?

Here! If I stand very still there's lots of light from the Budweiser sign.

Huh! Oh, Danny. Would I like to drink? A beer? I suppose a beer's fine. Should I have a beer? Sure.

TREVOR: What's that one doing? He's dashing about like a rat in a maze.

What's he looking at? Oh, he's all hot for the Steroid Set. God, who'd want them? You should sit here and hear them. All together they have the I.Q. of a Purdue chicken.

He shouldn't stand under that sign. It makes him look like a tomato with lips.

Oh, God, there's Cory. Where can I hide?

(He and CORY *exchange waves, as* CORY *takes a place at some distance.)*

What's he done to his head?

He didn't!

Wonder where the old dear trapped it? Makes him look like a spaniel in heat.

Good heavens, where did he come from? Well, God has bestowed a blessing on this dreary joint. How'd *he* find his way here? Lost, no doubt. Poor dear. I might just help him find his way safely back to my place. Delightful, and one of the few people I've ever seen who can wear yellow. Looks like cashmere.

Oh, Chris, another vodka and bitters and easier on the ice. Have Danny bring it to me over there.

(Moves to where new man stands and speaks to him.)

Isn't this just the dreariest lot you've ever laid eyes on?

CORY: I'll just hide...*wait*...here till Danny comes by. Oh, Trevor you old bitch, stop staring.

It feels straight. I walked very carefully.

Stop touching it. Keep your hands off it. You'll get it cockeyed and then what will you do?

I'm sure I can still smell the glue. How much Aramis does it take?

Now what's Trevor staring at? Good God, who wouldn't? Beautiful. Oh, to be ten years younger. Well, twenty. Be still my impetuous heart. I see Trevor's wasting no time. He'd have him down in a gulp. Wouldn't even spit up the shoelaces.

Was I ever young? Did beautiful men pursue me? Did I ever say no to someone my age? Yes, and may God forgive you for being so nasty to that nice old man. I'm too old for this place, too young for SAGE. I've never been the right age.

And what's wrong with old? People go for muscles...toes... feet...thumbs, noses...moustaches. There must be somebody who's crazy about wrinkles.

It moved. I'm sure it moved left. Stand very still...

Ah, Danny, a scotch and water when you...

Yes, Danny, it's me. Yes, isn't it. No, I wouldn't know me either.

The young have no tact.

(*Lights down, then up immediately.*)

NICK: He looks everywhere but here. I'm over here. The love of your life is twelve feet away under the Budweiser sign.

Maybe if I sit up straighter. Smile.

No! The trick is to look as if you're not interested in anything.

What is his type?

Maybe just a little frail, a little helpless...the kind a big man could take care of.

No, butch. His kind would like 'em butch.

I'd unbutton my shirt, but if he likes 'em hairy I'd...

Where'd *he* come from? *Yes*! But could I be untrue to Mr.

Muscles? Give up my true love for a beautiful man in a gorgeous yellow sweater?

God, yes!

Ah, Chris, bring me another beer. No, make that a double vodka on the rocks.

TREVOR: And just who the fucking hell does he think he is? "Thank you anyway, but I don't think I'll stay for another drink." Try to be sociable... He certainly looked a lot better from a distance. Must have had terrible acne as a child. Losing a few pounds wouldn't do him any harm either. I'm sure the sweater's orlon. Nineteen ninety-five at most. From K-Mart.

Look at this lot. Not a one I'd give the time of day to. Why do I bother?

Another, Chris. No ice.

CORY: It's heading towards my eyes. It will crawl right down my forehead and over my nose.

Oh, Jesus, just take it off and put it in your pocket.

But if I hurt it they won't give me my money back.

Can you kill a toupee?

NICK: Isn't he beautiful in that sweater?

Forgive me, Mr. Muscles, but I am about to be unfaithful.

What do I have to do to get his attention? Am I invisible?

No, there I am in the mirror.

(*Gives a small wave to himself.*)

Quick, say something or he'll get away.

That's the prettiest sweater I've ever seen. Where did you get it?

You knitted it?

Yeah, I'm here fairly often.

No, I don't think I know any Kurt.

You're welcome. Goodnight.

Oh, Mr. Muscles, forgive me. I wasn't really untrue. It was

just a moment of weakness.

TREVOR: Well, I've had almost enough to go over and be pleasant to poor old Cory. It will be my good deed for the day. I will say nothing about his new collection of hair. I will not stare, point or laugh. It will not be easy.

But it's late, and why not? He's not so bad. He could be worse. He could be more boring.

Chris! One for the road.

CORY: Just go over to him, young man. Don't just sit there and stare. You don't have forever.

I should start a school for the terminally young. Father Cory's School for Passive Pansies. How to Go Out and Get the Man of Your Dreams...and How to Get Rid of the Nightmares After You Get Them.

Huh? Just talking to myself, Danny. No, no more. Time to get the hell out of the old corral. 'Night.

NICK: He's seen me. He's smiling. He's...he's coming over.

I...I...He's bigger in person.

Mine's Nick.

Every Friday.

You fum here coffin? I mean...

I've wanted...

Sure I would. It's just I bruise so easy. The littlest bump.

If you'd just like to come by, we could...

Goodnight.

Maybe I should pee. Do I have to?

(*He runs off, runs back immediately.*)

Pleased to meet you.

(*He's halfway into a bow, but stops himself.*)

TREVOR: Well, it's time to be kind to Old Cory.

When did he...?

Already? For Christ's sake, Chris, don't turn the lights on.

Let me get safely away. Away from another night of broken dreams, of crushed...

No, I don't need help. Don't I always get out on my own.
Of course you'll see me tomorrow.
What would you do without me?

CODAS

THE COMPANY

ARNOLD:

(*He is holding something against his chest which can't be seen when he answers phone.*)

You're back. Good time? Everything's packed and ready, so you and Donny can... Oh? When? I see. He met him in St. Thomas. I see. The new apartment's in his name. I see. Then where are you living? Fred's. Ah! But you'd like to stay here? It's...difficult. How difficult? I mean it's out of the...There's this...I've sublet for a while. How long? Don't know. I'm going...I'm going to Mexico. Get some of your things? Sure. The yellow sweater? Yes. It's...look, I'm sorry. I wish I could, but... Thursday at one is fine. 'Bye.

(*Hangs up.*)

Too late.

(*Throws ball of yellow yarn in air and catches it.*)

DANA:

Here's the check, Geoffrey. Your people did a really wonderful job on the party. And please apologize to your waiter for me. Mr. Farringer had a little too much to drink. Still, he should never have said what he did to your man. Mrs. Clay should have gin spilled on her regularly. First time all night I was sure she was awake.

Oh, Geoffrey, you know I'd like to...I'd love to...but it's late and I can never be sure he'll stay asleep. What about your place tomorrow? Three? Three-thirty then? I'm free then...for all evening, if you can. Yes, oh yes, it will.

FRANCIS:

You startled me, father. Did the washing machine wake you up? I cut myself and got blood on the sheets. I didn't want it to set. Mrs. Cleary would be fit to be tied. All our fine old linen. You're right. This old machine would wake the dead. Let's pray it doesn't, huh? Can't think of many I'd like to see again. Yes, of course you're right, father. Yes, it was a bad joke. Of course I'll pray they're in God's hands, that we all are.

EDDIE:

I miss any action? The guy was OK. Yeah, he was nice looking. Over on Beekman. I see the Rabbit's in. He tried to stiff Bill. Jesus, will you look who's coming in: your friend The Drooler. You could have better than that, you do something 'bout your teeth. It'd be good for business. Jesus, what makes you think this ain't a business? Don't be dumb. Gotta run it like a business. See that slob over there? He look like he's got a hundred-fifty? He's got it, I'm going home with him. Prove a point. Money's money. That's all this is about, and don't forget it.

PHIL:

It's Phil, Fred. Come home. Please! Tell them you feel sick. My mother's answered my letter and I can't open it. I put it in the living room and now I can't even go in there. How do I know what it says? I told you, I can't go near it, so how do I know whether it's bad or good. And what would be bad or good? By now I don't know which I want. That's wrong. I do know. What I want is to care about people who care about me.

ONE ON ONE

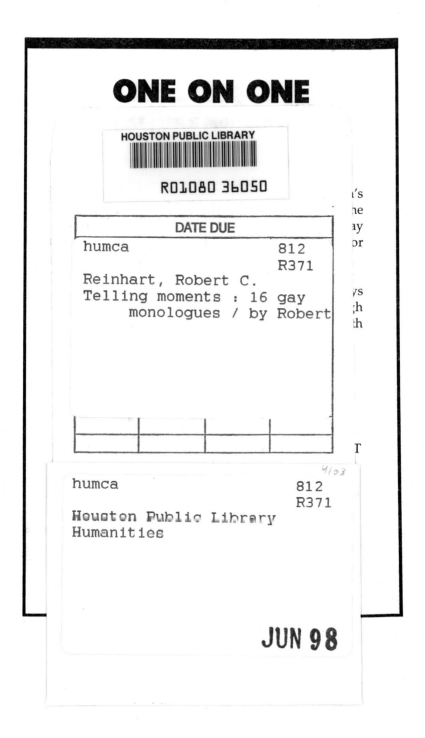